SUPER
SWEETS

SUPER SWEETS

Easy-to-Make Recipes for
Delicious Homemade Candy

HONEY AND LARRY ZISMAN

St. Martin's Press
New York

Design by Laura Hammond
ISBN: 0-312-77641-1

Library of Congress Catalog Number: 83-24518
First Edition

10 9 8 7 6 5 4 3 2 1

for Sam,
who would have loved them all

"SWEETS TO THE SWEET."

—William Shakespeare, *Hamlet*
Act V, Scene 1

CONTENTS

INTRODUCTION

There is no doubt about it—WE LIKE CANDY!

Every year in the United States all of us together eat nearly 4 billion pounds of candy costing over $7 billion.

That is a lot of candy.

Just like many other foods, candy tastes better if you make it yourself at home. There are reasons why restaurants advertise "Home Cooking" and packages in the supermarket say "Home Style" and "Just Like Home-made."

What you make at home is fresher, has finer ingredients, contains fewer additives and preservatives, and, frankly, tastes a whole lot better. In addition, you get a feeling of satisfaction knowing that you made it yourself rather than just buying it at the store.

Unfortunately, though, making your own candy at home has usually meant special thermometers and other equipment along with detailed instructions requiring exact temperatures and constant judging to determine if the candy mixture was at hard ball, soft crack, or some other precise point.

These intricate and exacting procedures, requiring specialized utensils, not only decreased the fun and increased the difficulty of making candy at home, but also kept many people from even trying.

HERE IS A WELCOME CHANGE.

In this book you will find easy recipes that everyone can follow using the regular utensils found in any kitchen. You will not need a candy thermometer, nor will you have to recognize firm ball, hard crack, or anything else you have never seen before.

AND YOU WILL BE MAKING ABSOLUTELY, POSITIVELY SCRUMPTIOUS HOMEMADE CANDY.

NOW READ, MAKE, EAT, AND ENJOY!

I

OLD TIME FAVORITES

TURKISH TAFFY

2 cups sugar
1/2 cup light corn syrup
1/2 cup water
2 egg whites
1 cup coarsely chopped pecans or walnuts
1 teaspoon vanilla

Grease a 1-inch band around the top inside rim of a heavy saucepan.

Combine sugar, corn syrup, and water in the saucepan and heat to boiling. Boil over medium high heat for 10 to 12 minutes.

Beat egg whites well.

Pour sugar mixture very slowly into egg whites, beating constantly, until mixture becomes very thick. Add pecans and vanilla, stirring well.

Drop by teaspoonfuls onto wax paper. Let sit in freezer until hard.

Store in freezer if hard candy is desired.

Store in refrigerator if chewy candy is desired.

Yield: approximately 4 dozen candies

*T*he earliest known candy making took place in the eastern Mediterranean area.

About 5,000 years ago, people living in Asia Minor enjoyed halvah, a confection made with honey and crushed sesame seeds and somewhat similar to the halvah of today.

A few hundred years later, the Egyptians began making candy by mixing together honey and various combinations of figs, dates, nuts, and spices. These mixtures were pressed into molds in the shape of geese, bulls, and obelisks and then brightly colored with dyes. Most of the candy was made in temples since it was to be offered to the gods and eaten by the priests and royalty.

There are many Egyptian tomb drawings, papyrus rolls, and hieroglyphics that tell about and show pictures of candy being made.

Following the Egyptians, the Greeks and Romans made candy with fruits, nuts, spices, and sweet herbs. Hippocrates, the famed Greek physician often called the "father of medicine," along with other Greek and Roman doctors, rubbed the rims of cups with candy to get patients to drink the bitter tasting medicines inside.

This practice probably was the origin of the phrase "using a sugar coating" to cover up anything disagreeable.

It was not until the fifteenth century that candy really started to be eaten just as a treat or a snack. Up to then, the primary use of candy was to disguise the unpleasant taste of medicines and candy was made and sold mostly by doctors and pharmacists.

HONEY PEANUT
CREAMS

1 cup creamy or chunky peanut butter
1 cup honey
2 cups instant nonfat dry-milk powder
1 1/4 cups confectioner's sugar

Combine all ingredients and knead until mixture is well blended.

Using slightly dampened hands, press mixture into a greased 8-inch square pan. Chill in refrigerator until firm.

Cut into small squares.

Yield: approximately 5 dozen squares

According to legend, Atlantic City's famous salt water taffy got its name in the summer of 1883 after a heavy storm sent the ocean crashing over the taffy stands on the boardwalk. The day after the storm a woman came up to one of the candy vendors and asked for some "salt water taffy" and the name stuck.

Now, a century later, more than 300,000 pounds of salt water taffy are sold each year in Atlantic City.

OLD-FASHIONED
SUGARPLUMS

2 cups coarsely chopped pitted dates
2 cups coarsely chopped figs
1 1/3 cups coarsely chopped raisins
1 cup coarsely chopped walnuts or almonds
1 cup coarsely chopped pistachio nuts
1/8 teaspoon ginger
1 1/2 tablespoons grated orange peel
brandy
confectioner's sugar

Combine dates, figs, raisins, walnuts, pistachio nuts, ginger, and orange peel. Mix together well. Add just enough brandy for mixture to stick together.

Shape mixture into 1-inch balls. Roll in sugar.

Yield: approximately 2 dozen candy balls

The English word candy *comes from the Sanskrit word* khanda, *meaning "a piece of broken sugar cane," and the Arabic word for sugar,* quand.

ALMOND ROCA

1 cup butter or margarine
³/4 cup coarsely chopped blanched almonds
1 ¹/4 cup sugar
1 cup (6 ounces) milk chocolate chips

Melt butter in a large heavy saucepan over low heat. Add almonds and sugar. Increase heat to high and continue cooking, stirring continuously and rapidly, until sugar melts and color of the mixture becomes light tan. Almonds will start to pop. Immediately remove from heat.

Pour mixture into a slightly warmed 9 × 13-inch pan, spreading mixture as evenly as possible to a thickness of about ³/8-inch. Mixture may not completely cover bottom of pan.

Sprinkle chocolate chips over hot mixture in pan and spread chocolate evenly after it has melted. Let cool.

Remove candy by inverting pan and hitting on bottom. Break mixture into small pieces with a heavy spoon.

Yield: approximately 8 dozen candies

FAMILY'S FAVORITE PEANUT BUTTER SQUARES

1 cup butter or margarine
1³/4 cups graham cracker crumbs
1 cup creamy or chunky peanut butter
2¹/4 cups confectioner's sugar
2 cups (12 ounces) semisweet chocolate chips

Melt butter over low heat. Combine melted butter, graham cracker crumbs, peanut butter, and sugar, mixing together until smooth. Press mixture into a 9 × 13-inch pan.

Melt chocolate chips over hot water, stirring until smooth. Pour melted chocolate over graham cracker mixture.

Chill in refrigerator until hard. Cut into squares.

Yield: approximately 5 dozen squares

GRAPE JELLIES

1/2 cup sugar
1 ounce unflavored gelatin
1/4 teaspoon salt
2 1/2 cups grape juice
sugar

Combine sugar, gelatin, and salt in a large bowl. Set aside.

Heat grape juice to boiling. Pour grape juice into sugar and gelatin mixture, stirring until mixture is completely dissolved. Pour mixture into a 9 × 13-inch pan. Let sit until firm.

Cut into small squares. Sprinkle sugar over squares.

Yield: approximately 8 dozen squares

When the children of Israel were traveling across the desert after fleeing from Egypt, they received manna from heaven to eat. As described in the Bible, Exodus, 16:31, the manna was "like coriander seed, white; and the taste of it was like wafers made with honey."

According to this Biblical description, manna was a light candy.

PECAN DIPS

4 egg yolks
²/₃ cup heavy cream
²/₃ cup sugar
2²/₃ cups (16 ounces) chocolate chips
6 tablespoons vegetable shortening
1 teaspoon vanilla
pecan halves

Beat egg yolks until thick. Add heavy cream and sugar. Heat over hot water until mixture becomes thick. Set aside.

Combine chocolate chips and shortening and heat over hot water, stirring until mixture has melted and it is smooth and well blended. Let cool slightly.

Add half of melted chocolate to egg yolk mixture. Add vanilla, beating together well. Chill in refrigerator until slightly firm.

Shape mixture into 1-inch balls. Place a pecan half on opposite sides of the candy balls. Dip in the remaining melted chocolate. Place on greased cookie sheet. Let cool.

Store in refrigerator.

Yield: approximately 3½ dozen candy balls

MINT SMOOTHIES

2²/₃ cups (16 ounces) milk chocolate chips
1 ounce baking chocolate
1 14-ounce can sweetened condensed milk
2 tablespoons butter or margarine
¹/₈ teaspoon peppermint extract
1 teaspoon vanilla

Combine the chocolates, milk, and butter and heat over hot water, stirring until mixture has melted and it is smooth and well blended. Add peppermint extract and vanilla, mixing well.

Pour mixture into a greased 8-inch square pan. Let cool. Cut into small squares.

Let sit in refrigerator for five days before serving.

Yield: approximately 5 dozen squares

One of the earliest books on candy making published in France was The French Confectioner, *written by a sixteenth-century physician and astrologer, Michel de Nostredame. He is better known today as Nostradamus, and for his prophecies rather than for his candies.*

CREAM CHEESE FUDGE

3 ounces softened cream cheese
2 1/2 cups confectioner's sugar
1/4 teaspoon almond extract
1/2 cup chopped walnuts or blanched almonds

Beat together cream cheese, sugar, and almond extract until smooth. Stir in walnuts. Press mixture into a greased 9-inch loaf pan.

Chill in refrigerator until firm. Cut into small squares. Store in refrigerator.

Yield: approximately 3 dozen squares

Around 1960, Ronald Reagan gave up smoking and began eating jelly beans instead. His fondness for those little candies became legend and for his inauguration as President of the United States on January 20, 1981, 32 million red (cherry), white (coconut), and blue (boysenberry) jelly beans were shared by those attending celebration parties in Washington.

COCONUT CHOCOLATE
PRINTS

½ cup butter or margarine
3 cups flaked coconut
2 cups confectioner's sugar
1 cup (6 ounces) semisweet chocolate chips

Melt butter over low heat. Remove from heat. Add coconut and sugar, mixing together well.

Shape mixture into 1-inch balls. Press thumb in center of each ball, making an indentation. If ball is too dry to hold shape when pressed with thumb, add a few drops of water and reshape into ball.

Place on a greased cookie sheet with indentation facing up. Set aside.

Melt chocolate chips over hot water, stirring until smooth. Place a teaspoonful of melted chocolate in each indentation.

Chill in refrigerator until firm. Store in refrigerator.

Yield: approximately 3 dozen candy balls

PEANUT BRITTLE

3/4 cup coarsely chopped peanuts
2 cups sugar

Spread peanuts in a greased pan. Set aside:

In a heavy saucepan cook sugar over high heat, stirring continuously and rapidly, until sugar dissolves and becomes a thin, light brown syrup.

Pour sugar over peanuts. Let sit until completely hard. Break into pieces.

Yield: approximately 4 dozen candies

*A*round 1890, a woman in New England was making peanut taffy in her kitchen where she had many unlabeled bottles and cans filled with cooking ingredients. By mistake she picked up the wrong container and added baking soda instead of cream of tartar to the syrup cooking on her stove.

The result was not the taffy she expected but a totally new candy creation now called peanut brittle.

FONDANT

4 1/2 cups sifted confectioner's sugar
1/3 cup butter or margarine
1/2 cup light corn syrup
1 teaspoon vanilla
food coloring (optional)
flavoring extract (optional)

Combine 2 cups of the sugar, butter, and corn syrup in a heavy saucepan and cook over low heat, stirring constantly, until mixture comes to a boil. Immediately add remaining sugar and vanilla. Remove from heat.

Stir mixture in saucepan until it holds its shape. Pour into a greased bowl. Let cool until mixture can be handled.

Knead mixture until smooth. If colored fondant is desired, add food coloring. If flavored fondant is desired, add flavoring extract. Shape candy into 1-inch balls.

Yield: approximately 3 1/2 dozen candy balls

(If desired, fondant balls can be dipped in melted chocolate.)

GRANDPOP'S MATZO FARFEL CANDY

1 1/4 cups honey
1 cup matzo farfel
3/4 cup slivered almonds
1/2 teaspoon ginger
1/2 cup wine or whisky

Put honey in a saucepan and heat to boiling. Add matzo farfel, almonds, and ginger. Simmer mixture for about 3 minutes until matzo farfel and almonds are well coated with honey.

Wet a bread board with water. Pour mixture onto bread board, spreading evenly to a thickness of about 1/4-inch. Coat top of candy with wine.

Score with knife into diamond shaped pieces. Chill in refrigerator until hard. Break apart along scored lines.

Yield: approximately 2 1/2 dozen candies

STRAWBERRIES

6 ounces strawberry flavored gelatin
1 cup pecan meal
1 cup flaked coconut
7 ounces sweetened condensed milk
1/2 teaspoon vanilla
slivered almonds
green food coloring
red sugar crystals

Combine gelatin, pecan meal, coconut, milk, and vanilla, kneading together well. Shape mixture into strawberries. Chill in refrigerator for 2 hours.

Tint slivered almonds with green food coloring. Set aside.

Roll strawberries in red sugar crystals.

Attach pieces of colored almonds to strawberries, forming leaves and stems.

Store in a cool place.

Yield: approximately 2 1/2 dozen candies

*T*ootsie Rolls were created in 1896 by Leo Hirschfield, a recent immigrant from Austria who had opened a small shop in New York City to make candies from recipes he had brought with him from Europe. He named his new candy after his six-year-old daughter, Clara, who was nicknamed, of course, "Tootsie."

Another Hirschfield innovation was to wrap each Tootsie Roll in paper to keep it clean, making it the first penny candy to be individually wrapped.

The Tootsie Roll of today is basically unchanged from the candy invented over 85 years ago by Mr. Hirschfield.

COCONUT PATTIE
SQUARES

1 cup (6 ounces) chocolate chips
2 tablespoons vegetable shortening
1 14-ounce can sweetened condensed milk
1/4 ounce unflavored gelatin
5 1/2 cups flaked coconut
1/2 cup chopped or slivered almonds

Combine chocolate chips and shortening and heat over hot water, stirring until mixture has melted and is smooth and well blended.

Spread half of the melted chocolate mixture in a greased 8-inch square pan. Chill in refrigerator until hard.

Combine milk and gelatin in a heavy saucepan and heat to boiling, stirring to dissolve gelatin. Remove from heat. Stir in coconut and almonds. Let cool to lukewarm.

Spread milk mixture evenly over chocolate in pan. Spread remaining half of chocolate mixture over milk mixture. Let cool until firm.

Cut into 2-inch squares. Wrap each square individually in plastic wrap or silver foil.

Yield: approximately 16 squares

LICORICE JELLY
SQUARES

³/₄ ounce unflavored gelatin
1 ¹/₄ cups water
2 cups sugar
¹/₂ teaspoon anise extract
sugar

Soften gelatin in ¹/₂ cup of the water. Set aside.

Heat the remaining ³/₄ cup of water to boiling. Add sugar and water with gelatin. Boil slowly for 15 minutes, stirring occasionally. Remove from heat. Stir in anise extract. Pour mixture into an 8-inch square glass pan. Let sit for 12 hours.

Cut into squares. Roll in sugar. Store in a covered container.

Yield: approximately 3¹/₂ dozen squares

Licorice is a perennial herb native to Southern Europe and parts of Asia. Over 40 million pounds of dried licorice root are shipped to the United States each year.

Licorice extract is used as a flavoring agent in soft drinks, liqueurs, cigarettes, and cigars; as a foaming agent for beer; and as an emulsifier in chocolates. After the flavoring extract is removed, the root fibers become ingredients in making fire-fighting foam, boxboard, and insulation board.

The early Chinese ate licorice to preserve their youth and strength while the Brahmans of India believed it to be both a tonic and a beautifier. Today, licorice is used as a soothing agent in cough drops, as a flavoring in unpleasant medicines, and in the treatment of peptic ulcers and Addison's disease, a disorder of the adrenal glands.

II

CHEWY AND CRUNCHY

PEANUT-CARAMEL BARS

2 cups (12 ounces) milk chocolate chips
2 tablespoons vegetable shortening
30 vanilla caramels
3 tablespoons butter or margarine
2 tablespoons water
1 cup coarsely chopped peanuts

Combine chocolate chips and shortening and melt over hot water, stirring until mixture is smooth and well blended. Pour half of the melted chocolate mixture into a greased 8-inch square pan, spreading evenly. Chill in refrigerator until firm.

Combine caramels, butter, and water and heat over hot water, stirring until mixture has melted and it is smooth and well blended. Stir in peanuts, mixing together well.

Pour caramel mixture over chocolate in pan, using dampened hands to spread caramel evenly. Chill in refrigerator until caramel mixture is tacky.

Remelt remaining chocolate mixture over hot water, stirring until smooth. Pour over caramels, spreading evenly. Chill in refrigerator until firm.

Cut into 1-inch by 2-inch bars. Store in refrigerator.

Yield: approximately 2½ dozen bars

CHEWY MOUNTAINS

36 vanilla caramels
1/3 cup milk
1 cup cornflakes cereal
1 cup crisp rice cereal
1 cup flaked coconut
1/2 cup chopped nuts

Combine caramels and milk and heat over hot water, stirring until mixture has melted and it is smooth and well blended. Stir in cereals, coconut, and nuts, mixing together well.

Drop by teaspoonfuls onto a greased cookie sheet. Let cool.

Yield: approximately 4 dozen candies

CORNFLAKES CANDY

3 tablespoons butter or margarine
1 1/4 cup brown sugar, firmly-packed
1/3 cup evaporated milk
5 cups cornflakes cereal

Melt butter in a heavy saucepan over low heat. Add sugar and mix together well. Slowly add milk, stirring constantly, until sugar has completely dissolved. Remove from heat. Add cereal, stirring until well mixed.

Using dampened hands, press mixture into a greased 8-inch square pan. Cover loosely with wax paper. Let sit in a cool, dry place for 2 days.

Break into small pieces.

Yield: approximately 4 cups of candy

In a move to make Cracker Jack more appealing to adult customers, in 1979 the company began putting more peanuts into every box.

CHOCO-MINT CRUNCHIES

2²/₃ cups (16 ounces) milk chocolate chips
¹/₂ cup crushed hard-peppermint candies
¹/₂ teaspoon peppermint extract

Melt chocolate chips over hot water, stirring until smooth. Remove from heat. Stir in peppermint candies and peppermint extract, mixing well. Pour mixture onto a greased cookie sheet, spreading out to a thickness of about ¹/₈-inch. Chill in refrigerator until firm.

Score into small squares. Chill in refrigerator until hard. Break apart along scored lines.

Yield: approximately 6 dozen squares

PEANUT BUTTER
TREATS

2 cups chunky peanut butter
2 tablespoons softened butter or margarine
1 1/4 cups sifted confectioner's sugar
3 cups crisp rice cereal
4 teaspoons light corn syrup

Blend together peanut butter and butter. Stir in sugar. Add cereal and corn syrup, mixing well. Press mixture into a lightly greased 8-inch square pan. Chill in refrigerator.

Cut into squares.

Yield: approximately 5 dozen squares

(If desired, melted chocolate can be spooned over candy squares.)

According to the Guinness Book of World Records, *Life Savers are the best-selling candy of all time. More than 30 billion rolls—containing 340 billion little circles of candy—have been sold in the last 70 years.*

CEREAL CRUNCH

2 cups cornflakes cereal
1 cup crisp rice cereal
1/2 cup (3 ounces) chocolate chips
1/2 cup coarsely chopped pecans
1/2 cup coarsely chopped walnuts
3/4 cup dark corn syrup
1/4 cup sugar
2 tablespoons butter or margarine
1/2 teaspoon vanilla

Mix together cereals, chocolate chips, and nuts. Set aside.

In a heavy saucepan combine corn syrup, sugar, and butter. Cook over medium heat and boil for 3 minutes, stirring continuously. Let cool for about 10 minutes.

Add vanilla to corn syrup and sugar mixture, beating until mixture turns light brown in color and becomes thick. Pour over cereals, chocolate chips and nuts, stirring to coat completely with syrup.

Using dampened hands, press mixture into a greased 8-inch square pan. Chill in refrigerator until firm.

Cut into squares. Store in a tightly covered container.

Yield: approximately 2 1/2 dozen squares

CARAMEL
TURTLES

24 soft caramels
2 tablespoons frozen whipped topping
72 pecan halves
2/3 cup (4 ounces) semisweet chocolate chips

Combine caramels and whipped topping and heat over hot water, stirring until mixture has melted and it is smooth and well blended. Let cool slightly.

Place pecan halves on a lightly greased cookie sheet in groups of 3, arranged such that one pecan half is in the position of a turtle's head while the other 2 pecan halves are in the position of the turtle's legs on each side.

Carefully spoon the melted caramels over each group of 3 pecan halves, leaving the ends of the pecan halves showing. Let sit until hard.

Melt chocolate chips over hot water, stirring until smooth. Let cool slightly.

Spoon melted chocolate over caramel topping on pecan halves, taking care not to cover the pecan heads and legs of the turtles. Let sit until hard.

Yield: 2 dozen candies

CRISPY MALLO-RICE

4 tablespoons butter or margarine
4 cups miniature marshmallows
5 cups crisp rice cereal or other crisp cereal

Melt butter in a large saucepan over low heat. Add marshmallows, stirring until mixture is melted and well blended. Remove from heat. Add cereal, blending well until cereal is coated with marshmallow mixture. Press into a greased 9 × 13-inch pan. Let cool completely. Cut into 2-inch squares.

Yield: approximately 2½ dozen squares

Caramels were invented by accident by a candy maker in Chicago who added cream to a butterscotch mixture he was preparing in an experiment to improve the flavor and texture. He soon discovered that he had not merely improved the butterscotch but that he had, in fact, created a whole new type of candy.

For a while after they first appeared, caramels were used mainly as a summer replacement for chocolate when the weather got too hot for making and storing chocolate.

PEANUT BUTTER-OATMEAL
ROUNDS

2 cups sugar
1/2 cup milk
1/8 teaspoon salt
1/2 cup chopped nuts
1/2 cup creamy or chunky peanut butter
1/4 cup unsweetened cocoa powder
4 tablespoons softened butter or margarine
3 cups uncooked quick-oat cereal
1 teaspoon vanilla

Combine sugar, milk, and salt. Boil for 1 minute while stirring. Remove from heat. Add nuts, peanut butter, cocoa powder, butter, oatmeal, and vanilla, mixing together well. Drop by teaspoonfuls onto a greased cookie sheet. Let cool.

Store in a covered container.

Yield: approximately 4 dozen candies

PEANUT CHEWS

²/₃ cup evaporated milk
1¹/₃ cups sugar
10 caramels
1 cup (6 ounces) chocolate chips
1¹/₃ cups salted peanuts
flaked coconut

Combine milk, sugar, and caramels and heat to boiling. Continue boiling, stirring often, until caramels have melted. Add chocolate chips and cook until chocolate chips have melted. Let cool until thick.

Add peanuts, stirring together well. Chill in refrigerator for about 1 hour.

Drop by rounded teaspoonfuls into coconut. Shape into balls. Chill in refrigerator.

Store in a tightly covered container.

Yield: approximately 4 dozen candy balls

PEANUT BUTTER CUPS

2 cups (12 ounces) semisweet chocolate chips
1 cup (6 ounces) milk chocolate chips
2 tablespoons butter or margarine
1 cup creamy peanut butter
16 cupcake papers

Combine chocolate chips and butter and melt over hot water, stirring until mixture is smooth and well blended. Set aside.

Melt peanut butter over hot water, stirring until smooth.

Place a tablespoon of melted chocolate mixture into each of 16 cupcake papers. Let cool.

Place a tablespoon of melted peanut butter over the chocolate in the cupcake papers. Let cool.

Place a tablespoon of melted chocolate mixture over each peanut butter layer in the cupcake papers. Let cool completely.

Store in a cool place.

Yield: 16 candies

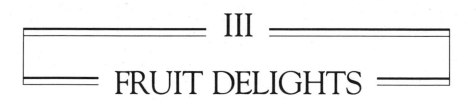

III

FRUIT DELIGHTS

PEANUT BUTTER
FRUITS

1/2 cup creamy peanut butter
1/2 cup finely chopped figs
1/2 cup finely chopped prunes
1/4 cup finely chopped dried apricots
1/4 cup finely chopped dried pears
1/4 cup finely chopped dried peaches
1 cup granola
1/2 cup slivered almonds
1 tablespoon light corn syrup
1/2 cup (3 ounces) milk chocolate chips (optional)
confectioner's sugar

Mix together peanut butter, figs, prunes, apricots, pears, peaches, granola, almonds, and corn syrup. Combine well.

If chocolate is desired, melt chocolate chips over hot water, stirring until smooth. Add to fruit and peanut butter mixture, blending in well.

Using slightly dampened hands, shape mixture into 1/2-inch balls. Roll in confectioner's sugar.

Yield: approximately 3 1/2 dozen candy balls

SPICED FRUIT BALLS

1 cup chopped pecans
3/4 cup chopped dried apricots
1 cup chopped pitted dates
3 1/2 cups graham-cracker crumbs
1 cup marshmallow creme
1 tablespoon grated orange peel
1/4 cup orange juice
1/4 teaspoon ground cinnamon
1/4 teaspoon nutmeg
1/4 teaspoon cloves
1/4 teaspoon allspice
1/4 teaspoon ginger
confectioner's sugar

Mix together pecans, apricots, dates, and graham-cracker crumbs. Set aside.

Combine marshmallow creme, orange peel, orange juice, cinnamon, nutmeg, cloves, allspice, and ginger. Cook over low heat, stirring until mixture has melted and it is smooth and well blended.

Pour marshmallow creme mixture over pecan and fruit mixture, blending together well.

Using dampened hands, shape mixture into 1-inch balls. Roll in confectioner's sugar.

Store in a tightly covered container.

Yield: approximately 5 dozen candy balls

During a coin shortage in Italy, storekeepers in Rome, Florence, and other cities gave small pieces of candy to customers as change instead of 10-lira coins (worth about a penny). In place of the scarce coins, candy was kept in the cash register bins designated for 10-lira pieces.

RASPBERRY NUT
GEMS

2 cups frozen red raspberries, drained
1 1/2 tablespoons grated orange peel
3/4 cup orange juice
1 ounce unflavored gelatin
1 1/2 cups sugar
1 cup chopped walnuts

Combine raspberries, orange peel, and orange juice in a large saucepan. Cook mixture for about 5 minutes.

Force mixture through a fine strainer. Save the liquid. Discard the residue left in the strainer.

Combine strained raspberry liquid, gelatin, and sugar in a saucepan. Stir until sugar is dissolved. Cook over medium heat, stirring often, for about 5 minutes. Remove from heat. Add walnuts and mix together well.

Spread candy evenly in a greased 9-inch loaf pan. Let sit for 12 to 24 hours.

Cut into small squares. Let sit on a wire rack for 12 to 24 hours.

Yield: approximately 3 dozen squares

MEG'S FRUIT BITES

1 cup granola
1/2 cup chopped figs
1/4 cup finely chopped dried apricots
1/4 cup finely chopped dried pears
1/4 cup finely chopped dried peaches
1/2 cup coarsely chopped walnuts
1/4 cup coarsely chopped pistachio nuts
2 tablespoons orange juice
1 teaspoon lemon juice
1/2 teaspoon grated orange peel
flaked coconut

Mix together well granola, figs, apricots, pears, peaches, walnuts, pistachio nuts, orange juice, lemon juice, and orange peel.

Using slightly dampened hands, shape mixture into 1/2-inch balls. Roll in coconut.

Yield: approximately 3 1/2 dozen candy balls

CANDIED ORANGE OR GRAPEFRUIT PEELS

4 oranges
cold water
1 cup sugar
1/2 cup water
sugar

Wipe off oranges well. Cut oranges into quarters. Remove peels. Cut peels into narrow strips.

Put orange peels in a saucepan and cover with cold water. Heat to boiling. Drain water, leaving peels in saucepan. Again cover peels with cold water and heat to boiling. Drain water, leaving peels in saucepan.

Repeat this process 6 more times.

Combine sugar and 1/2 cup water in a saucepan. Heat until sugar has completely dissolved. Add orange peels. Cook slowly until syrup has almost completely disappeared. Remove from heat. Drain any remaining syrup.

Roll peels in sugar. Place on a lightly greased cookie sheet. Let cool.

(For making Candied Grapefruit Peels, peel grapefruits, weigh peels, and use an equal amount of sugar and follow the same procedures for making Candied Orange Peels.)

Yield: approximately 6 dozen slices

*T*he lollipop was invented around 1850 by a pencil manufacturer who saw children chewing on the ends of their pencils. He introduced a pencil with a small block of sugar candy on the end.

The first lollipop-making machine was produced by the Racine Confectioners' Machinery Company in Racine, Wisconsin. It could turn out 40 lollipops every minute, a rate its manufacturer believed would produce more lollipops in one week than could be sold in an entire year.

PEANUT BUTTER
DATES

pitted dates
creamy or chunky peanut butter
sugar

Cut each date lengthwise forming a pocket in the date. Fill pocket in date with peanut butter. Close up pocket. Roll in sugar.

Place on a greased cookie sheet. Chill in refrigerator.

Store in refrigerator in a closed container.

Yield: as many dates as desired

TANGERINE DREAMS

2 tangerines
1 1/3 cups confectioner's sugar
1 teaspoon lemon juice
confectioner's sugar

Grate peels from the tangerines.

Mix together grated peels, sugar, and lemon juice. Set aside.

Squeeze juice from the tangerines into a bowl.

Add tangerine juice, a little at a time while stirring, to grated peel mixture, until mixture becomes a stiff paste.

Shape into 1-inch balls. Roll in sugar.

Store in refrigerator.

Yield: approximately 2 1/2 dozen candy balls

APPLE CINNAMON
SLICES

3 firm apples
1 cup sugar
3/4 cup water
2 tablespoons red cinnamon candies
sugar

Peel apples. Cut into quarters. Remove core. Cut each quarter into 3 slices. Set aside.

Combine sugar and 1/2 cup of the water in a small saucepan and heat to boiling. Boil for 5 minutes. Add cinnamon candies.

Drop 12 apple slices into sugar mixture. Cook over low heat until apple slices become transparent. Remove from sugar mixture. Place on a greased cookie sheet. Set aside.

Add half of the remaining 1/4 cup of water to sugar mixture in saucepan. Drop in 12 more apple slices. Cook apple slices until they, too, become transparent. Remove from sugar mixture. Place on a greased cookie sheet. Set aside.

Add remaining water to saucepan. Cook the last 12 apple slices until they become transparent. Remove from sugar mixture. Place on a greased cookie sheet.

Let all the apple slices sit for 24 hours in a cool place. Roll in sugar.
Let sit for another 24 hours in a cool place. Roll in sugar again. Let sit until completely dry.

Yield: 3 dozen candies

More candy is made in the United States than in any other country in the world.

PECAN AND RAISIN
BARS

1 cup (6 ounces) milk chocolate chips
1 cup (6 ounces) semisweet chocolate chips
1 tablespoon vegetable shortening
2/3 cup chopped pecans
1/2 cup raisins

Combine chocolate chips and shortening and heat over hot water, stirring until mixture has melted and it is smooth and well blended. Set aside.

Spread pecans and raisins in the bottom of a well greased 9-inch loaf pan.

Gently pour melted chocolate mixture over pecans and raisins in pan. Chill in refrigerator until hard.

Cut into bars.

Yield: approximately 18 bars

*N*early $2 billion worth of candy bars are eaten in the United States each year.

CHERRY TREATS

1 cup miniature marshmallows
1 cup (6 ounces) semisweet chocolate chips
1/2 cup flaked coconut
20 maraschino cherries cut into quarters

Evenly distribute marshmallows in the bottom of a greased 9-inch loaf pan. Set aside.

Melt chocolate chips over hot water, stirring until smooth. Pour melted chocolate over marshmallows.

Sprinkle coconut and cherry pieces over chocolate and press firmly with hands. Let sit until hard.

Run a knife around edge of mixture in loaf pan and gently lift out. Cut into small squares.

Yield: approximately 3 dozen squares

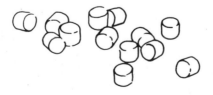

CHOCOLATE-COATED
RAISINS

2 cups raisins
flour
1 cup (6 ounces) milk chocolate chips
1 tablespoon vegetable shortening

Chill raisins in freezer for 2 hours.

Lightly coat raisins with flour. Set aside.

Combine chocolate chips and shortening and melt over hot water, stirring until mixture is smooth and well blended.

Drop raisins in melted chocolate all at once, stirring to coat completely. Using a slotted spoon, remove raisins from chocolate, letting excess chocolate drip back.

Place coated raisins on a greased cookie sheet and separate with a fork. Chill in refrigerator.

Remove from cookie sheet with a dull knife or spatula.

Yield: approximately 2 cups of raisins

IV

KIDS' FAVORITES

CARAMEL CORN

2 cups light brown sugar
1/2 cup light corn syrup
1 cup butter or margarine
1/2 teaspoon cream of tartar
1 teaspoon baking soda
16 cups lightly salted popcorn
1 cup peanuts

In a heavy saucepan combine sugar, corn syrup, butter, and cream of tartar and dissolve over low heat. Bring mixture to a boil and continue boiling for 10 to 12 minutes over medium heat, stirring often. Remove from heat. Add baking soda, mixing well. Mixture will foam and turn light tan in color.

Place popcorn and peanuts in a large bowl. Pour sugar mixture over popcorn and peanuts, stirring until completely coated.

Spread coated popcorn and peanuts in a large greased roasting pan.

Bake at 250°F for about 45 minutes, stirring often. Let cool.

Yield: approximately 17 cups of caramel corn

OVERNIGHT DELIGHT
PECAN ROLL

3³/₄ cups graham-cracker crumbs
1 14-ounce can sweetened condensed milk
5 cups miniature marshmallows
1 cup chopped pecans

Combine graham-cracker crumbs and milk. Add marshmallows and pecans, mixing together well. Shape mixture into a large ball. Using slightly dampened hands, shape ball into a long roll.

Wrap roll in plastic wrap. Chill in refrigerator for 12 to 24 hours.

Slice roll into ¹/₄-inch slices. Store in refrigerator in a tightly covered container.

Yield: approximately 4 dozen slices

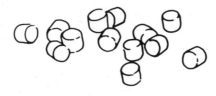

COCONUT POPCORN BALLS

2 cups (12 ounces) milk chocolate chips
1/2 cup corn syrup
2 tablespoons water
4 cups popcorn
1 cup chopped nuts
flaked coconut

Combine chocolate chips, corn syrup, and water and heat over hot water, stirring until mixture has melted and it is smooth and well blended. Set aside.

Mix together popcorn and nuts in a large bowl.

Pour melted chocolate mixture over popcorn and nuts, stirring well to coat popcorn and nuts completely with chocolate.

Using greased hands, shape mixture into 11/2-inch balls. Roll in coconut.

Place on a greased cookie sheet. Let sit until firm. Store in refrigerator.

Yield: approximately 2 1/2 dozen candy balls

CHOCOLATE-COVERED
PRETZELS

2 cups (12 ounces) chocolate chips
2 tablespoons vegetable shortening
36 pretzels

Combine chocolate chips and shortening and melt over hot water, stirring until mixture is smooth and well blended.

Dip pretzels, one at a time, in melted chocolate, coating both sides of the pretzels.

Place on wax paper. Chill in refrigerator until hard.

Yield: 3 dozen pretzels

Clarence A. Crane invented Life Savers candy out of necessity rather than by choice or design. He was using a machine owned by a pill manufacturer to press out hard-candy mints that he was selling. Because of a defect in the machine, it worked better if a hole were punched out in the center of each mint.

Making the best of the situation, he called them "Crane's Life Savers" and the rest, as they say, is history.

FABULOUS PEANUT
CRUNCH

3/4 cup creamy peanut butter
1 cup light corn syrup
1 cup (6 ounces) milk chocolate chips

Put peanut butter in a bowl. Set aside.

Boil corn syrup in a small saucepan until it turns golden brown in color. Pour over peanut butter and mix at medium speed with an electric mixer until peanut butter and corn syrup are well blended. Immediately remove mixture from bowl and, using wet hands, press mixture into a greased 9 × 13-inch pan. Let cool.

Melt chocolate chips over hot water, stirring until smooth. Spread half of melted chocolate over peanut butter mixture in pan. Let sit until completely hard.

Turn mixture over in pan. Spread other side with remaining half of melted chocolate. Let cool completely.

Break into bite-sized pieces.

Yield: approximately 6 dozen candies

CHOCOLATE MINIROLLS

1 ounce baking chocolate
1 tablespoon butter or margarine
1/2 cup corn syrup
1/2 teaspoon vanilla
1/3 cup instant nonfat dry-milk powder
1 1/2 cups confectioner's sugar
confectioner's sugar

Combine chocolate and butter and melt over hot water, stirring until mixture is smooth and well blended. Stir in corn syrup and vanilla. Remove from heat. Add milk powder and sugar, mixing together until it is hard to stir.

Place mixture on a smooth counter top that has been lightly sprinkled with sugar. Knead until smooth and easy to roll out. Divide mixture into 4 parts.

Shape each part into a 12-inch long roll. Cut rolls into 2-inch lengths. Wrap each candy individually in plastic wrap. Store in refrigerator.

Yield: approximately 2 dozen candies

PEANUT BUTTER
WHATEVERS

½ cup plus 1 tablespoon butter or margarine
2 cups creamy natural peanut butter
2 cups confectioner's sugar
1 cup (6 ounces) chocolate chips
1 cup (6 ounces) butterscotch chips

Blend together ½ cup of the butter and all of the peanut butter. Add sugar and knead well. Press mixture into a 9 × 13-inch pan. Smooth out top of mixture with a flat knife or a spatula. Set aside.

Combine chocolate and butterscotch chips and remaining tablespoon of butter and heat over hot water, stirring until mixture has melted and is smooth and well blended.

Spread chip mixture evenly over top of peanut butter mixture. Chill in refrigerator until partially firm.

Cut into small squares. Refrigerate until completely firm.

Store in refrigerator.

Yield: approximately 8 dozen squares

JORDANA'S THREE-LAYER SQUARES

1 egg
1 cup plus 2 tablespoons butter or margarine
1/4 cup granulated sugar
1/4 cup unsweetened cocoa powder
1 teaspoon vanilla
2 cups graham-cracker crumbs
1 cup flaked coconut
3 tablespoons milk
3 ounces instant vanilla pudding mix
2 cups confectioner's sugar
1 cup (6 ounces) chocolate chips

Lightly beat egg. Set aside.

Combine 1/2 cup of the butter with granulated sugar, cocoa powder, and vanilla and heat over hot water until butter melts. Stir in egg. Cook until mixture hardens. Blend in graham-cracker crumbs and coconut. Press mixture into a 9 × 13-inch pan. Set aside.

Cream 1/2 cup of the butter. Beat in milk, vanilla pudding mix, and confectioner's sugar, continuing to beat until mixture becomes fluffy. Spread evenly over graham cracker-crumb mixture in pan. Chill in refrigerator until firm.

Combine chocolate chips and the remaining 2 tablespoons of butter and melt over hot water, stirring until mixture is smooth and well blended. Spread melted chocolate evenly over mixture in pan.

Cut into small squares. Store in refrigerator.

Yield: approximately 8 dozen squares

Cadbury, the British candy company, got an unusual surprise one year from its cream-filled chocolate Easter eggs.

Twenty-five million of them were packed and ready for shipment when they started exploding, sending chocolate and cream flying all over the packing cases. It seems that an extra strong yeast had been used in making the cream filling and that the material had fermented and expanded, shattering the chocolate eggs.

Nearly a million dollars of candy was ruined and there was a shortage of chocolate Easter eggs in Great Britain. All was not lost, however, since some of the damaged candy was used as cattle feed.

BUTTERSCOTCH PEANUT
BARS

1 cup (6 ounces) butterscotch chips
1/4 cup shortening
1/2 cup confectioner's sugar
1 cup Spanish peanuts
1 cup slightly crushed chow mein noodles
2 cups (12 ounces) chocolate chips

Combine butterscotch chips and half of the shortening and melt over hot water, stirring until mixture is smooth and well blended. Stir in sugar, peanuts, and noodles. Let cool to lukewarm.

Combine chocolate chips and remaining shortening and melt over hot water, stirring until mixture is smooth and well blended.

Spread half of melted chocolate mixture on a greased cookie sheet covering the area of an 8-inch square. Chill in refrigerator until firm.

Spoon butterscotch mixture over chocolate on cookie sheet, spreading to make an even layer. Smooth out top and edges of butterscotch layer.

Spread remaining half of chocolate mixture over butterscotch layer, covering it completely. Chill in refrigerator until firm.

Cut into 1-inch by 2-inch bars. Wrap each bar individually in plastic wrap or silver foil.

Yield: approximately 2 1/2 dozen bars

CHOCOLATE-COVERED MARSHMALLOWS

1 1/3 cups (8 ounces) milk chocolate chips
1 teaspoon solid vegetable shortening
20 marshmallows
3/4 cup finely chopped nuts or pecan meal

Combine chocolate chips and shortening and melt over hot water, stirring until mixture is smooth and well blended. Let cool slightly.

Place a toothpick in the center of each marshmallow and dip the marshmallows, one at a time, in the melted chocolate. Completely cover each marshmallow.

Roll marshmallows in nuts. Place on a greased cookie sheet. Chill in refrigerator for 20 minutes.

Yield: 20 marshmallows

One chocolate chip contains enough food energy for an adult to walk 150 feet. The 675 chocolate chips in a 12-ounce package have the food energy required for that same adult to walk 19 miles.

SWEET TREAT
BUTTERSCOTCH LOG

1 1/2 cups (9 ounces) butterscotch chips
7 ounces sweetened condensed milk
1/2 teaspoon vanilla
1/3 cup finely chopped hazelnuts
coarsely chopped hazelnuts

Melt butterscotch chips over hot water, stirring until smooth. Remove from heat. Add milk and vanilla, stirring well. Add finely chopped hazelnuts and mix well. Chill in refrigerator for 15 minutes.

Using slightly dampened hands, shape mixture into a roll about 12 inches long. Cover roll with coarsely chopped hazelnuts. Wrap roll in plastic wrap. Chill in refrigerator.

Cut into 1/2-inch slices. Store in refrigerator.

Yield: approximately 2 dozen slices

The two "M"s in "M&M"s come from the names of Forrest E. Mars and Bruce Murrie, the original partners of M&M Limited, a candy company founded in Newark, New Jersey, over 40 years ago.

CARAMEL BALLS

2 cups marshmallow creme
3 1/2 cups confectioner's sugar
1 teaspoon vanilla
1/4 teaspoon almond extract
48 soft caramels
finely chopped pecans or pecan meal

Combine marshmallow creme, sugar, vanilla, and almond extract, mixing together well.

Using slightly dampened hands, divide mixture into 8 equal parts. Shape each part into a 1-inch diameter roll. Wrap rolls in wax paper. Place in freezer for 12 to 24 hours.

Melt caramels over hot water, stirring until smooth. Keep caramels over hot water.

Dip marshmallow rolls into melted caramels. Coat rolls with pecans, pressing nuts firmly into rolls. Let cool.

Cut rolls into 1/2-inch slices. Shape slices into balls. Roll candy balls in pecans. Store in a cool, dry place.

Yield: approximately 4 dozen candy balls

MARSHMALLOW CHIP
BARS

2 cups (12 ounces) chocolate chips
2 cups (12 ounces) butterscotch chips
1 cup chunky peanut butter
7 cups miniature marshmallows
2 cups Spanish peanuts

Combine chocolate chips, butterscotch chips, and peanut butter and melt over hot water, stirring until mixture is smooth and well blended. Let cool slightly. Stir in marshmallows and peanuts.

Spread mixture in a greased 9 × 13-inch pan. Let cool completely. Cut into small bars.

Yield: approximately 6 dozen bars

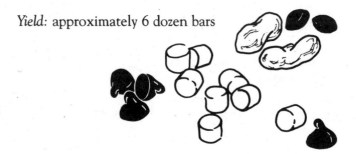

PEANUT BUTTER CREAM
FUDGE

1/2 cup (3 ounces) semisweet chocolate chips
2 cups (12 ounces) butterscotch chips
7 ounces sweetened condensed milk
1/2 cup creamy peanut butter
1/2 cup chopped pecans

Combine chocolate chips and butterscotch chips and melt over hot water, stirring until mixture is smooth and well blended. Remove from heat. Stir in milk, peanut butter, and pecans, mixing together well. Pour mixture into a greased 8-inch square pan.

Chill in refrigerator. Cut into small squares.

Yield: approximately 5 dozen squares

Marshmallow candy was first made by the Egyptians who used the dried and pulverized roots of the marsh mallow plant.

It was believed that marshmallows cured chest ailments and pharmacists offered them as a remedy for breathing problems.

ROCKY ROAD PEANUT BUTTER DROPS

2 cups (12 ounces) butterscotch chips
1 cup creamy peanut butter
1/2 cup butter or margarine
3/4 cup flaked coconut
3 cups miniature marshmallows
1/2 cup chopped walnuts

Combine butterscotch chips, peanut butter, and butter and melt over hot water, stirring until mixture is smooth and well blended. Let cool about 10 minutes.

Add coconut, marshmallows, and walnuts, mixing together well.

Drop by teaspoonfuls onto a greased cookie sheet. Chill in refrigerator until hard.

Yield: approximately 4 dozen candies

FUDGE GRAHAM
SQUARES

2 cups sugar
1/2 cup butter or margarine
1 cup cream or evaporated milk
1 cup (6 ounces) chocolate chips
3/4 cup flour
1 cup graham-cracker crumbs
3/4 cup coarsely chopped walnuts
1 teaspoon vanilla

In a heavy saucepan combine sugar, butter, and cream. Heat mixture and let boil for 10 minutes, stirring often. Add chocolate chips, flour, graham-cracker crumbs, walnuts, and vanilla. Stir until mixture becomes thick.

Using dampened hands, press mixture into a greased 8-inch square pan. Chill in refrigerator. Cut into squares.

Yield: approximately 3 dozen squares

*J*ust as caramels were an accidental invention when some butterscotch was being made, another candy was created during the preparation of a batch of caramels.

In a candy shop in Philadelphia in the late 1800s, something went wrong with a caramel mixture as it was being cooked. Instead of becoming chewy, it developed a finely crystalized texture. The head cook tasted the supposedly ruined candy and exclaimed, "Fudge! Bah!" and added a new word—and a new treat—to the world of candy.

MARSHMALLOW
BUMPIES

3 ounces softened cream cheese
2 tablespoons milk
2 cups confectioner's sugar
1/4 teaspoon vanilla
2 ounces baking chocolate
1/8 teaspoon salt
3 cups miniature marshmallows
flaked coconut

Blend together cream cheese and milk. Add sugar and vanilla, mixing well. Set aside.

Melt chocolate over hot water, stirring until smooth.

Combine cream cheese mixture, melted chocolate, and salt, mixing together well. Fold in marshmallows.

Drop by teaspoonfuls into coconut, completely coating each candy. Place on a greased cookie sheet. Chill in refrigerator until firm.

Yield: approximately 5 dozen candies

PEANUT BUTTER
FUDGE

3 ounces softened cream cheese
2 tablespoons creamy peanut butter
2¹/₂ cups sifted confectioner's sugar
1 teaspoon vanilla
¹/₂ cup chopped salted peanuts

Combine cream cheese and peanut butter, mixing together until soft and smooth. Blend in sugar. Add vanilla and peanuts. Knead until well mixed.

Press mixture into a well greased 8-inch square pan. Chill in refrigerator until firm. Cut into small squares.

Yield: approximately 5 dozen squares

There are now about 600 different toy surprises included in Cracker Jack boxes but in the Spring of 1983 some customers got startling surprises they never expected when they opened the boxes. Instead of finding a toy or game, they discovered a tiny illustrated booklet with the title "Erotic Sexual Positions from Around the World." Apparently, one of the Cracker Jack employees decided to liven up the prizes without consulting anyone else in the company.

V

FOR CHOCOLATE
LOVERS

CRAIG'S CHOCOLATE TRUFFLES

8 ounces baking chocolate
4 ounces sweet chocolate
2 tablespoons sugar
1/2 teaspoon cinnamon
1 14-ounce can sweetened condensed milk
finely chopped walnuts

Melt the chocolates over hot water, stirring until smooth. Add sugar, cinnamon, and milk, mixing together until very smooth. Let cool slightly.

Shape mixture into 1-inch balls. Roll in walnuts. Chill in refrigerator. Store in refrigerator in a tightly covered container.

Yield: approximately 4 dozen candy balls

Chocolate truffle candy gets its name from its bumpy surface and dusty cocoa coating that resemble the expensive eatable truffle fungus that is rooted out of the ground by trained dogs and pigs.

SOPHISTICATED
CHOCOLATE DROPS

1 cup (6 ounces) semisweet chocolate chips
3 tablespoons butter or margarine
2 teaspoons grated orange peel
1 egg

Combine chocolate chips and butter and melt over hot water, stirring until mixture is smooth and well blended. Add orange peel and mix well.

Beat egg.

Stir the chocolate mixture, a little at a time, into the beaten egg. Mix together well.

Drop by teaspoonfuls onto a greased cookie sheet. Chill until firm.

Yield: approximately 2 dozen candies

During World War II the Hershey Chocolate Company produced Field Ration D, a special 4-ounce, 600-calorie quick energy candy bar. It was a combination of chocolate and other ingredients and resisted melting when carried around in a soldier's pocket.

Hershey made 12 million Field Ration D candy bars each day.

HONEY'S BEST-EVER
CHOCOLATE FUDGE

4 ounces baking chocolate
3¹/₃ cups (20 ounces) semisweet chocolate chips
2 cups marshmallow creme
1 cup finely chopped almonds or walnuts
4 cups sugar
¹/₄ teaspoon salt
2 tablespoons butter or margarine
1¹/₂ cups evaporated milk
2 tablespoons dark rum

Coarsely chop baking chocolate.

Place baking chocolate, chocolate chips, marshmallow creme, and almonds in a large mixing bowl. Set aside.

In a heavy saucepan combine sugar, salt, butter, and milk. Heat slowly to a boil, stirring constantly. Simmer for about 6 minutes.

Pour sugar mixture over chocolate mixture, add rum, and stir vigorously until mixture has melted and it is smooth and well blended.

Pour into a greased 9- × 13-inch pan. Smooth out top of mixture. Let cool until completely firm.

Cut into small squares. Store in a cool place.

Yield: approximately 8 dozen squares

CONTINENTAL TRUFFLES

1 cup (6 ounces) semisweet chocolate chips
3 tablespoons unsalted (sweet) butter or margarine
2 tablespoons confectioner's sugar
3 egg yolks
1 tablespoon rum
unsweetened cocoa powder

Melt chocolate chips over hot water, stirring until smooth. Mix in butter and sugar, continuing to stir until sugar dissolves. Remove from heat. Add egg yolks, one at a time, beating each one in well before adding the next one. Stir in rum.

Pour mixture into a bowl. Cover with wax paper. Let sit for 12 to 24 hours in a cool, dry place. Do not place in refrigerator.

Shape mixture into 1-inch balls. Roll candy balls in cocoa powder.

Yield: approximately 2½ dozen candy balls

WHITE CHOCOLATE
CRUNCH

¹/₄ *cup slivered almonds*
1 cup peanuts
1 cup sugared crisp cereal
1 cup crisp rice cereal
1 cup miniature marshmallows
16 ounces white chocolate

Spread almonds on a cookie sheet and bake in the oven at 325°F for 8 minutes.

Mix together almonds, peanuts, cereals, and marshmallows. Set aside.

Melt chocolate over hot water, stirring until smooth. Pour melted chocolate over nut and cereal mixture, stirring well.

Drop by teaspoonfuls onto a greased cookie sheet. Let sit until firm.

Yield: approximately 5 dozen candies

DOUBLE FUDGE

  2 cups brown sugar, firmly packed
  1 cup granulated sugar
  1 cup evaporated milk
  1 teaspoon cream of tartar
  1/2 cup butter or margarine
  2 cups marshmallow creme
  1 teaspoon vanilla
  1 cup (6 ounces) butterscotch chips
  1 cup coarsely chopped walnuts
  1 cup (6 ounces) chocolate chips

Combine sugars, milk, cream of tartar, and butter in a heavy saucepan. Cook over medium heat, stirring constantly, until mixture comes to a boil. Let cool for about 10 minutes, stirring occasionally.

Add marshmallow creme and vanilla, mixing together well.

Combine butterscotch chips and 1/2 cup of the walnuts to 2 cups of the sugar and marshmallow creme mixture, mixing together well.

Pour butterscotch mixture into a greased 8-inch square pan. Set aside.

Combine chocolate chips and remaining 1/2 cup of the walnuts to remaining sugar and marshmallow creme mixture, mixing together well. Pour chocolate mixture over butterscotch mixture in pan.

Chill in refrigerator until firm. Cut into small squares.

Yield: approximately 5 dozen squares

RUM TRUFFLES

2 cups (12 ounces) milk chocolate chips
1/3 cup butter or margarine
1/4 cup heavy cream
1 tablespoon rum
flaked coconut

Combine chocolate chips, butter, and cream and melt over hot water, stirring until mixture is smooth and well blended. Stir in rum. Chill in refrigerator until almost hard.

Drop by teaspoonfuls into coconut. Shape into 1-inch balls.

Yield: approximately 3 dozen candy balls

The Baby Ruth candy bar was not named after the great home-run king of the New York Yankees. It was named for President Grover Cleveland's daughter, Ruth, who was born in the White House in 1891 while her father was president. In fact, when Babe Ruth set out to promote his own Babe Ruth Home Run Candy Bar, the Curtiss Candy Company, the makers of Baby Ruth, got a legal order from the United States Patent Office preventing Babe Ruth from getting into the candy business.

CHOCOLATE DIANES

12 ounces dark sweet chocolate
3 tablespoons corn syrup
3 tablespoons evaporated milk
1/8 teaspoon salt
1/2 cup chopped nuts

Melt chocolate over hot water, stirring until smooth. Remove from heat. Add corn syrup, milk, and salt, mixing together well. Stir in nuts.
Using dampened hands, shape mixture into 1-inch balls. Place on a greased cookie sheet. Let sit until firm.

Yield: approximately 3 dozen candy balls

The Nestlé Company, which created the first chocolate chip about 45 years ago, now makes more than 50 billion of them each year.

CHOCOLATE MARSHMALLOW
CANDY

2 cups (12 ounces) semisweet chocolate chips
1/3 cup (2 ounces) milk chocolate chips
2 ounces baking chocolate
7 cups colored miniature marshmallows
1/4 cup chopped almonds

Melt the chocolates over hot water, stirring until smooth. Stir in marshmallows and almonds. Pour mixture into a greased 9-inch loaf pan. Chill in refrigerator until firm. Cut into small squares.

Yield: approximately 3 dozen squares

The largest candy bar ever made was a 3,100 pound Clark Bar that was exhibited in 1982 at the Kennywood Amusement Park near Pittsburgh, Pennsylvania, where the D. L. Clark Company is located. It was 15 feet long, 20 inches thick, and the size of about 19,000 regular Clark Bars.

ESTHER'S CHOCOLATE
CRUNCHIES

2 cups (12 ounces) semisweet chocolate chips or
  1 cup (6 ounces) semisweet chocolate chips and
  1 cup (6 ounces) butterscotch chips
1 1/2 cups crushed rice noodles
3/4 cup pecan meal or crushed Grape-Nuts cereal

Melt chocolate chips over hot water, stirring until smooth. Add noodles and pecan meal, mixing together well. Let cool slightly.

Spread mixture on a greased cookie sheet to a thickness of between 1/4- and 1/2-inch. Score mixture with a knife into bite-sized pieces. Chill in refrigerator until hard.

Break apart along scored lines. Store in refrigerator.

Yield: approximately 4 dozen candies

The best selling candies in the United States are, in order:

1. Snickers
2. M&M Plain and M&M Peanut
3. Hershey's Milk Chocolate with Almonds, Reese's Peanut Butter Cups, and Three Musketeers
4. Hershey's Milk Chocolate, Kit Kat, and Milky Way
5. Butterfinger, Mars Bar, and Twix
6. Almond Joy, Baby Ruth, Nestlé Crunch, and Watchamacallit

VI

AFTER-DINNER TREATS

PECAN BRANDY
AFTER-DINNER TREATS

1 cup (6 ounces) semisweet chocolate chips
³/₄ cup evaporated milk
2¹/₂ cups crushed vanilla wafers
¹/₂ cup confectioner's sugar
1 cup chopped pecans
¹/₃ cup apricot brandy
pecan meal or very finely chopped pecans

Combine chocolate chips and milk and heat over hot water, stirring until mixture has melted and it is smooth and well blended. Remove from heat. Add vanilla wafers, sugar, chopped pecans, and apricot brandy, mixing together well. Let cool for about 30 minutes.

Using dampened hands, shape mixture into 1-inch balls. Roll in pecan meal.

Chill in refrigerator until firm. Store in tightly covered container.

Yield: approximately 3 dozen candy balls

SUGAR-COATED NUTS

2 cups walnut halves
1 1/2 cups pecan halves
1 cup cashews
2 cups granulated sugar
1 cup water
1/2 teaspoon cinnamon

Place all ingredients in a heavy saucepan and mix together well. Cook over medium heat until all the water has disappeared and nuts look sugary.

Place nuts on a greased cookie sheet and quickly separate with a fork. Let cool.

Yield: approximately 6 cups of nuts

COFFEE-SCOTCH
SQUARES

2 cups (12 ounces) butterscotch chips
1 14-ounce can sweetened condensed milk
2 teaspoons vanilla
2 cups miniature marshmallows
1 cup chopped walnuts
2 cups (12 ounces) chocolate chips
2 teaspoons instant coffee powder

Melt butterscotch chips over hot water, stirring until smooth. Remove from heat. Stir in half of the milk and 1 teaspoon of vanilla. Pour mixture into a greased 9 × 13-inch pan, spreading evenly.

Sprinkle marshmallows and walnuts over butterscotch mixture in pan, pressing them lightly into the butterscotch.

Melt chocolate chips over hot water, stirring until smooth. Stir in coffee powder, remaining milk, and remaining vanilla. Spread chocolate mixture evenly over marshmallows and walnuts.

Chill in refrigerator until firm. Cut into 2-inch squares. Store in tightly covered container.

Yield: approximately 2½ dozen squares

MACADAMIA DROPS

1 1/3 cups (8 ounces) semisweet chocolate chips
1 14-ounce can sweetened condensed milk
2 cups macadamia nut halves

Melt chocolate chips over hot water, stirring until smooth. Stir in milk, mixing together well. Fold in macadamia nuts.

Drop by teaspoonfuls onto a greased cookie sheet. Let sit until hard.

Yield: approximately 5 dozen candies

Mocha is the name of a town in southwestern Yemen on the Red Sea about 45 miles north of the Bab el Mandeb Strait. A distinctive type of coffee was grown near the town and shipped from there during the sixteenth and seventeenth centuries when Mocha was a busy seaport.

This coffee became known as "mocha" coffee and, later, mocha was the name given to the mixture of this coffee and cocoa or chocolate.

BRANDY-COATED
ALMONDS

2 1/2 cups blanched almonds
3/4 cup butter or margarine
3 cups confectioner's sugar
1/2 cup brandy

Spread almonds on a cookie sheet and bake in the oven at 325° F for 12 minutes. Set aside.

Put butter, sugar, and brandy in a bowl and beat with an electric mixer until mixture is smooth and well blended.

Coat almonds with brandy mixture. Place on a greased cookie sheet. Let sit for 12 to 24 hours in a cool place.

Yield: approximately 2 1/2 cups of nuts

COFFEE LIQUEUR
TRUFFLES

1 1/3 cups confectioner's sugar
1/2 cup softened butter or margarine
1 1/3 cups (8 ounces) semisweet chocolate chips
1 1/2 teaspoons coffee liqueur
unsweetened cocoa powder

Combine sugar and butter, beating together until mixture becomes a paste. Set aside.

Melt chocolate chips over hot water, stirring until smooth. Let cool slightly.

Beat coffee liqueur into melted chocolate. Add sugar and butter mixture, beating well. Stir mixture until it is thick and cool and can be worked with hands.

Using dampened hands, shape mixture into 1-inch balls. Roll in cocoa powder. Chill in refrigerator until firm.

Store in refrigerator.

Yield: approximately 3 1/2 dozen candy balls

MINTY CREAM CHEESE
ROUNDS

6 ounces softened cream cheese
2 tablespoons softened butter or margarine
3½ cups confectioner's sugar
½ teaspoon peppermint extract
food coloring (optional)
granulated sugar

Blend together cream cheese and butter until smooth. Add confectioner's sugar and mix well. Mix in peppermint and, if desired, food coloring. Chill in refrigerator until firm.

Shape mixture into 1-inch balls. Roll in granulated sugar.

Using the bottom of a drinking glass that has been dipped in sugar, slightly flatten the candy balls. Store in refrigerator in a covered container.

Yield: approximately 2 dozen candies

ALMOND NUGGETS

1 1/3 cups (8 ounces) semisweet chocolate chips or
sweet chocolate
1/4 cup evaporated milk
1/4 cup crushed ginger snaps
1/4 cup confectioner's sugar
1/4 cup slivered almonds
1/2 teaspoon almond extract

Melt chocolate chips over hot water, stirring until smooth. Stir in milk, ginger snaps, sugar, almonds, and almond extract. Mix together well.

Drop by teaspoonfuls onto a greased cookie sheet. Let cool.

Let sit in a tightly covered container for 3 days before serving.

Yield: approximately 2 dozen candies

BOURBON BALLS

1 cup finely chopped pecans
2 cups crushed vanilla wafers
1 cup confectioner's sugar
1 1/2 tablespoons unsweetened cocoa powder
3 tablespoons light corn syrup
1/2 cup bourbon
confectioner's sugar

Combine pecans, vanilla wafers, sugar, cocoa powder, corn syrup, and bourbon, mixing together well.

Using slightly dampened hands, shape mixture into 3/4-inch balls. Roll candy balls in sugar.

Store in a tightly covered container.

Yield: approximately 3 1/2 dozen candy balls

Tiffany & Company, the exclusive jewelry store, offered for sale a gold chain with a set of four pendants, each one a replica of a Life Savers candy in a different flavor.

RUM ROUNDS

2 ounces semisweet chocolate
1 1/2 cups pecan meal
1 cup granulated sugar
1 egg white
2 tablespoons rum
confectioner's sugar

Grate chocolate.

Mix together grated chocolate, pecan meal, granulated sugar, egg white, and rum.

Using very wet hands, shape mixture into 1-inch balls. Roll candy balls in confectioner's sugar.

Let sit for 2 to 3 days in a warm place until dry.

Yield: approximately 2 dozen candy balls

PEPPERMINT PILLOWS

1 egg white
2 to 3 cups sifted confectioner's sugar
1/8 teaspoon peppermint extract
confectioner's sugar

Lightly beat egg white.

Stir together egg white and 2 cups of the sugar. Add peppermint extract. Continue stirring, adding more sugar as needed, until mixture becomes a stiff paste.

Place mixture on a smooth counter top that has been sprinkled with sugar. Divide mixture into 3 parts. Shape each part into a 1-inch diameter roll.

Cut rolls into 1/2-inch slices. Let sit in a cool place until hard.

Yield: approximately 8 dozen slices

THREE-NUT TOFFEE

6 ounces sweet chocolate
1/2 cup water
2 cups butter or margarine
2 tablespoons corn syrup
2 cups sugar
1 cup chopped almonds
1/4 cup chopped pecans
1/4 cup chopped walnuts

Grate chocolate. Set aside.

In a heavy saucepan combine water, butter, corn syrup, sugar, and almonds. Cook over high heat until mixture begins to smoke and turns tan in color. Pour mixture onto a greased cookie sheet.

Sprinkle grated chocolate, pecans, and walnuts over top of mixture. Let cool completely.

Break into pieces.

Yield: approximately 8 dozen candies

GRAHAM-CRACKER
BOURBON BALLS

1 cup graham-cracker crumbs
1 cup chopped walnuts
2½ tablespoons unsweetened cocoa powder
1 cup confectioner's sugar
1½ tablespoons light corn syrup
¼ cup bourbon
confectioner's sugar

Combine graham-cracker crumbs, walnuts, cocoa powder, sugar, corn syrup, and bourbon. Mix together well.

Shape mixture into ½-inch balls. Roll in sugar. Chill in refrigerator. Roll in sugar once more.

Store in refrigerator in a tightly covered container.

Yield: approximately 2½ dozen candy balls

MAPLE DROPS

1 egg white
2 to 3 cups confectioner's sugar
1/4 teaspoon cream of tartar
1 tablespoon softened butter or margarine
1 teaspoon maple flavoring
pecan halves

Combine in a bowl egg white, 2 cups of sugar, and cream of tartar. Add butter and maple flavoring, mixing well. Continue mixing, adding a little sugar at a time, until mixture becomes a stiff paste.

Using slightly dampened hands, shape mixture into 1-inch balls. Gently flatten candy balls. Place a pecan half on each flattened side.

Store in refrigerator in a tightly covered container.

Yield: approximately 2 dozen candy balls

The name "confetti" for the bits and pieces of paper thrown in celebration comes from the small, hard Italian candy of that name that carnival goers threw at each other back in the Middle Ages.

MOM'S HAZELNUT COFFEE
BONBONS

> 1 cup hazelnuts
> 2 tablespoons coffee liqueur
> 2 tablespoons very strong coffee
> 2 1/4 cups confectioner's sugar
> 4 ounces sweet chocolate
> 1/4 cup milk

Grind up the hazelnuts until a paste is formed. Mix together hazelnut paste, coffee liqueur, coffee, and sugar. Knead until smooth. Shape mixture into 1-inch balls. Chill in refrigerator for 1 hour.

Combine chocolate and milk and heat over hot water, stirring until mixture has melted and it is smooth and well blended.

Dip candy balls in melted chocolate. Place on wax paper. Let sit until firm.

Yield: approximately 3 dozen candy balls

In the "Question and Answer" column in the science section of The New York Times, *a reader asked why you can see sparks in your mouth in a darkened room when you crush wintergreen Life Savers with your teeth. The answer is that the sugar crystals in the candy give off a dim light when broken under pressure in a phenomenon called "triboluminescence," from the Greek word* tribein, *meaning "to rub."*

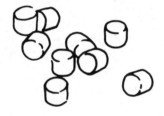

INDEX